The TECHNIQUE *of the* FLUTE

Chord Studies
Rhythm Studies

...ph Viola

BERKLEE PRESS

Editor in Chief: Jonathan Feist
Senior Vice President of Online Learning and Continuing Education/CEO of Berklee Online: Debbie Cavalier
Vice President of Enrollment Marketing and Management: Mike King
Vice President of Online Education: Carin Nuernberg
Editorial Assistants: Emily Jones, Eloise Kelsey, Megan Richardson
Cover Design: Ranya Karifilly

ISBN 978-1-4950-8692-2

Berklee
Press

1140 Boylston Street
Boston, MA 02215-3693 USA
(617) 747-2146

Visit Berklee Press Online at
www.berkleepress.com

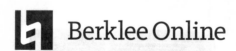

Berklee Online

Study music online at
online.berklee.edu

DISTRIBUTED BY

HAL•LEONARD®
7777 W. BLUEMOUND RD. P.O. BOX 13819
MILWAUKEE, WISCONSIN 53213

Visit Hal Leonard Online
www.halleonard.com

CONTENTS

FOREWORD: By Matt Marvuglio iv

BOOK I. CHORD STUDIES 1
    SECTION I. Studies on Chord Structures... 3
    Studies on Individual Chords 3
        Structures on C 3
        Structures on F... 13
        Structures on G.. 22
        Structures on B♭..31
        Structures on D.. 40
        Structures on E♭... 49
        Structures on A 58
        Structures on A♭... 67
        Structures on E 76
        Structures on Db... 85
        Structures on B 94
        Structures on G♭ 103
        Structures on F♯ 112
        Structures on C♭ 121
        Structures on C♯.. 130
    Summary Studies 139
    SECTION II. Studies on Chord Sequences 145

BOOK II. RHYTHM STUDIES.. 167
    SECTION I. Simple Meters 169
    SECTION II. Simple and Compound Meters 230
    SECTION III. Double-Time Exercises 250
    SECTION IV. Etudes 261
        Etude 1 262
        Etude 2 264
        Etude 3 267
        Etude 4 268
        Etude 5 269
        Etude 6 270
        Etude 7 274
        Etude 8 278
        Etude 9 280
        Etude 10.. 282
        Etude 11.. 284
        Etude 12.. 286
        Etude 13.. 286
        Etude 14.. 288

ABOUT THE AUTHOR 289

FOREWORD

Welcome to Joseph Viola's *Technique of the Flute*. Originally, this material was published as two separate volumes: *Chord Studies* and *Rhythm Studies*. Over the years, it became common for teachers to combine the two volumes so flutists could practice chord studies and rhythm studies in one practice session. This book provides the flutist with the harmonic and rhythmic vocabulary necessary for improvisation in a number of popular styles. The articulation patterns throughout the book are used in jazz, Latin, and other popular contemporary music styles. You will find that this approach is different from many of the classical flute technique books and many jazz improvisation books.

The chord studies should be practiced where you learn the patterns using at least three modalities: the fingering patterns, the sound of the chord, and how the pattern looks on paper. Each exercise begins with the basic chord pattern. Approach note patterns in diatonic and chromatic combinations are added to each chord tone, which creates a tension-resolution pattern. This is where you will be practicing your ear training. Listening to the different approach patterns and how they resolve to the chord tones (unstable-stable) will help you memorize these chords. This is a style of improvisation that is not touched upon in many improvisation methods. Eventually, you will be able to memorize these various chord patterns and improvise your own patterns by linking different chord changes together.

The rhythm studies are designed to teach a legato-staccato style of playing, which is the rhythmic language of jazz and other contemporary styles. For example, the eighth-note pickup to a quarter note would be long-short, or "Doo-Dot." Flutists studying classical music are brought up on a staccato-legato style of playing. The repertoire has this singing style throughout common practice music. The eighth-note pickup to a quarter note in a classical approach would be played "Dot-Doo." This notion will be illustrated throughout the rhythm studies exercises.

These rhythm studies are written in a format to help students with their sight-reading. In jazz and theater music, many examples are written in cut time. At the beginning of the rhythm portion of this book, each example is written two different ways: in time and in cut time. Make sure you read both examples. It's important to see what cut-time examples look like and how they feel. If you practice the chord studies and rhythm studies on a daily basis, you will build a rich harmonic vocabulary with a rhythmic sense that is syncopated and grooves at different tempos and in different styles. To practice the duets independently, record yourself playing both parts (use a metronome/click), and then play along with your recorded part.

Once you learn three chord patterns (say C, F, and G), try improvising a C blues with a play-along. Be conscious of the tempo and rhythmic feel and see if you can hook up with the band. Another application would be to take a tune that has diatonic chord changes, such as "Autumn Leaves," and play your diatonic triads in different rhythmic patterns along with the track. With any technique book, you need to find the practical applications for the techniques. Read melodies from lead sheets that have no articulations and add articulations and rhythms to make the melodies swing. You may also try embellishing a standard tune melody with chord tones and approach notes. These are just a few of the applications of the materials in this book. I hope you have fun exploring the different music possibilities this book has to offer.

Matt Marvuglio

Dean of Performance, Berklee College of Music

Boston, 2017

BOOK I

Chord Studies

To derive the most benefit from the "Chord Studies" exercises, it is important that the following practice procedure be followed with each new chord covered in Section I.

A. PREPARATORY EXERCISES

1. Play the basic chord (1, 3, 5 or 1, 3, 5, 7) several times until the tonality is firmly fixed in your ear.

2. Add high degrees one at a time. Try to hear the relationship of each tension to the basic chord.

3. Where altered tensions are indicated, relate each altered form to the basic chord.

B. EXERCISES EMPLOYING CHORD TONES AND AUXILIARY TONES
(Exercises 1, 2, and 3 of each chord)

1. Listen for the resolution of each auxiliary tone as it moves into the basic chord tone.

2. After repeating each exercise several times, play it without looking at the music. Concentrate on remembering the chord tones and let your ear assist you in finding the proper auxiliary tones.

C. EXERCISES EMPLOYING LOW DEGREE CHORD TONES, HIGH DEGREE CHORD TONES, AND AUXILIARY TONES
(Exercises 4 and 5 of each chord)

1. Be aware of the tonality of the basic chord at all times. If the tonality seems vague, stop and play the basic chord several times before repeating the exercise.

2. Experiment with various articulations. Suggested variations are indicated below.

All of the exercises may (and should) be played at different tempos and with variations in phrasing and interpretation.

The augmented chord has not been included since it is considered to be an altered form of the dominant seven.

—Joseph Viola, 1975

Studies on Chord Structures

STUDIES ON INDIVIDUAL CHORDS

Structures on C

C MAJOR

3

4

5

C MINOR

C SEVEN

C MINOR SEVEN

C MINOR SEVEN FLAT FIVE

C DIMINISHED SEVEN

Structures on F

F MAJOR

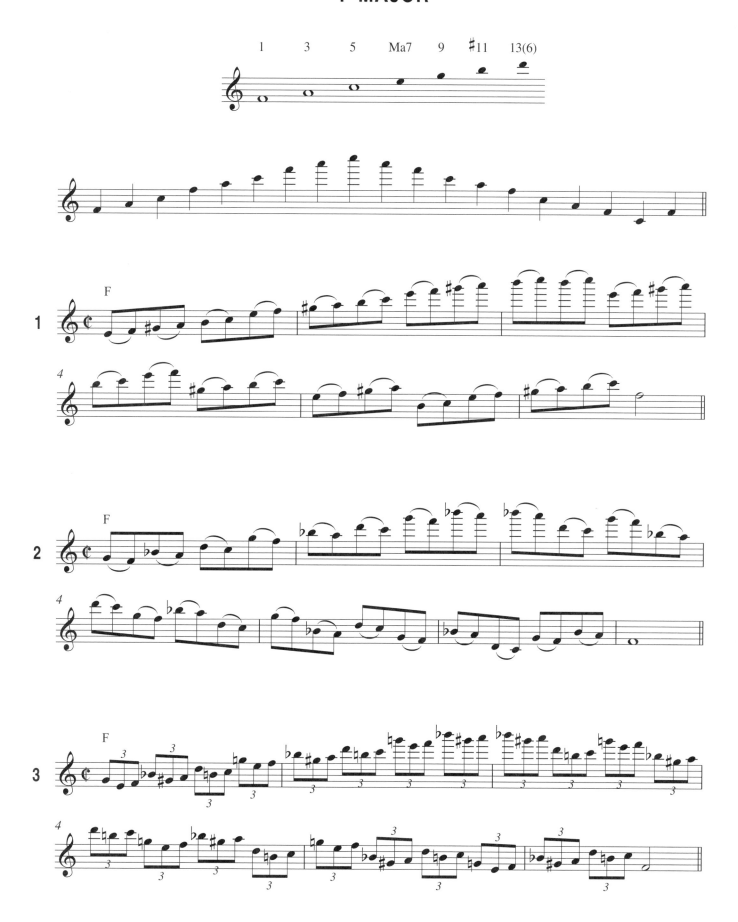

F MINOR

F SEVEN

F MINOR SEVEN

F MINOR SEVEN FLAT FIVE

F DIMINISHED SEVEN

Structures on G

G MAJOR

G MINOR

G SEVEN

G MINOR SEVEN

G MINOR SEVEN FLAT FIVE

G DIMINISHED SEVEN

Structures on B♭

B♭ MAJOR

B♭ MINOR

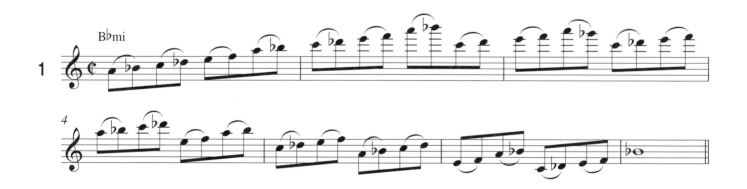

B♭ SEVEN

B♭ MINOR SEVEN

B♭ MINOR SEVEN FLAT FIVE

B♭ DIMINISHED SEVEN

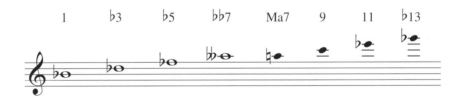

Structures on D

D MAJOR

D MINOR

D SEVEN

D MINOR SEVEN

D MINOR SEVEN FLAT FIVE

D DIMINISHED SEVEN

Structures on E♭

E♭ MAJOR

4

5

E♭ MINOR

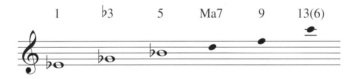

1

E♭ SEVEN

E♭ MINOR SEVEN

E♭ MINOR SEVEN FLAT FIVE

E♭ DIMINISHED SEVEN

Structures on A

A MAJOR

A MINOR

A SEVEN

A MINOR SEVEN

A MINOR SEVEN FLAT FIVE

A DIMINISHED SEVEN

Structures on A♭

A♭ MAJOR

A♭ MINOR

A♭ SEVEN

A♭ MINOR SEVEN

A♭ MINOR SEVEN FLAT FIVE

Ab DIMINISHED SEVEN

Structures on E

E MAJOR

E MINOR

E SEVEN

4

5

E MINOR SEVEN

1

E MINOR SEVEN FLAT FIVE

E DIMINISHED SEVEN

Structures on D♭

D♭ MAJOR

4

5

D♭ MINOR

1

D♭ SEVEN

Db MINOR SEVEN

Db MINOR SEVEN FLAT FIVE

4 Db mi7b5

5 Db mi7b5

Db DIMINISHED SEVEN

1 Db°7
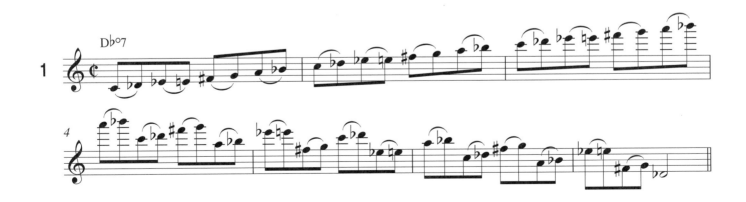

Structures on B

B MAJOR

B MINOR

B SEVEN

B MINOR SEVEN

B MINOR SEVEN FLAT FIVE

B DIMINISHED SEVEN

Structures on G♭

G♭ MAJOR

G♭ MINOR

G♭ SEVEN

Gb MINOR SEVEN

G♭ MINOR SEVEN FLAT FIVE

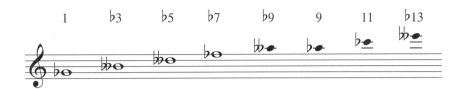

Gb DIMINISHED SEVEN

Structures on F♯

F♯ MAJOR

F♯ MINOR

F♯ SEVEN

F♯ MINOR SEVEN

F# MINOR SEVEN FLAT FIVE

F# DIMINISHED SEVEN

Structures on C♭

C♭ MAJOR

Cb MINOR

Cb SEVEN

4

3

5

3

Cb MINOR SEVEN

1

4

C♭ MINOR SEVEN FLAT FIVE

C♭ DIMINISHED SEVEN

Structures on C♯

C♯ MAJOR

C# MINOR

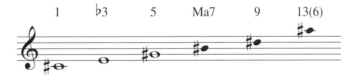

C♯ SEVEN

C# MINOR SEVEN FLAT FIVE

C# DIMINISHED SEVEN

SUMMARY STUDIES

Play all exercises an octave higher the second time through.

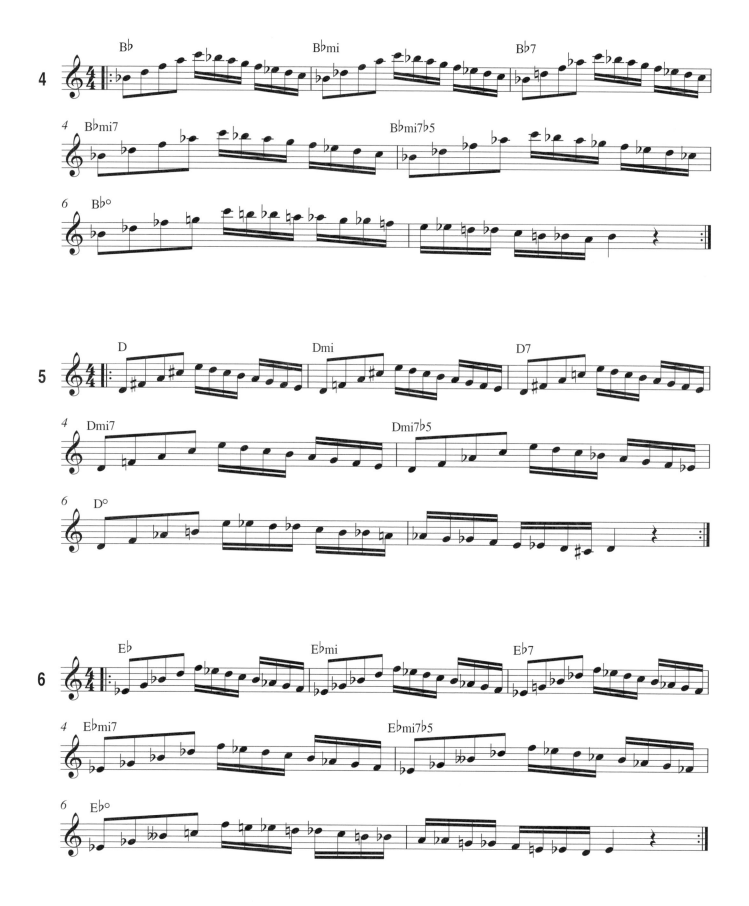

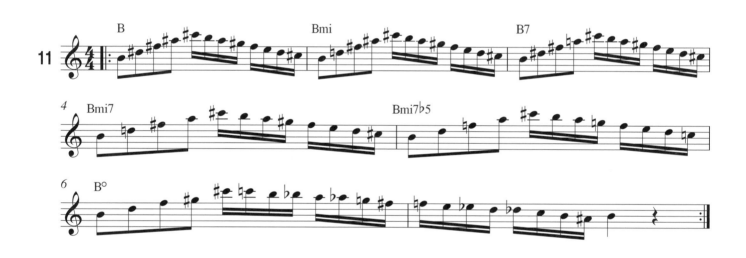

Studies on
Chord Sequences

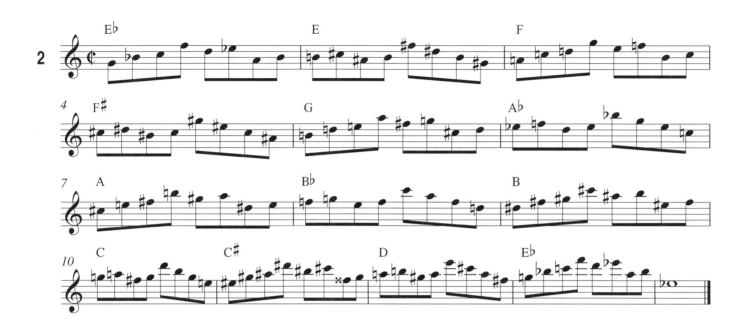

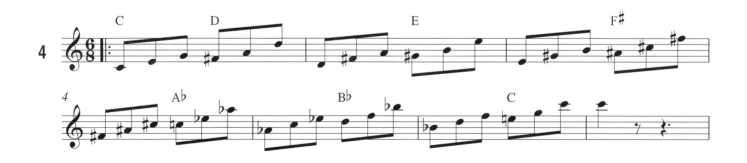

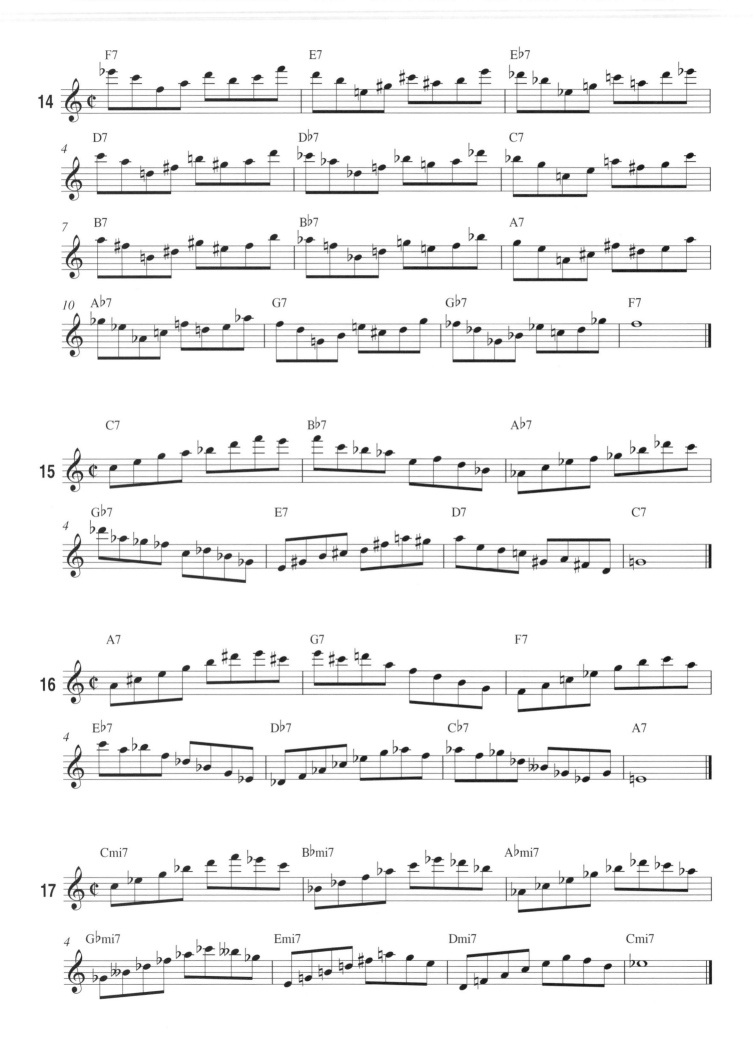

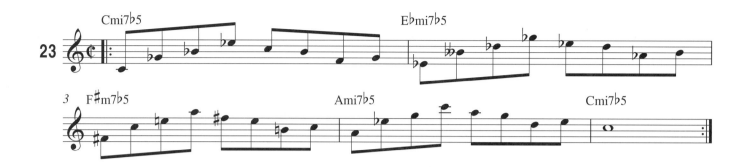

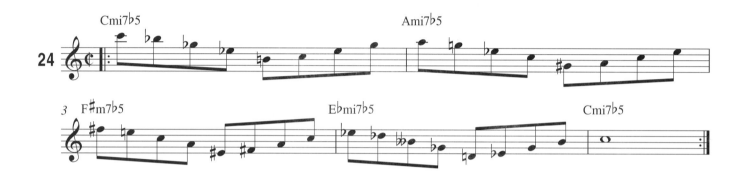

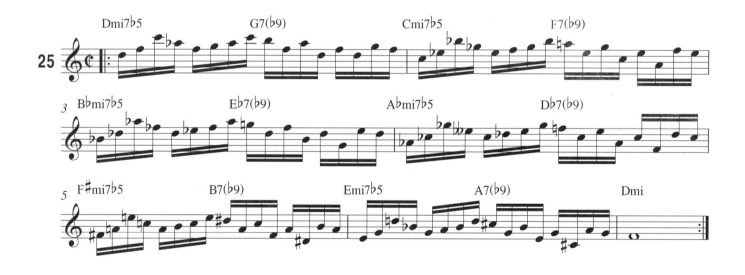

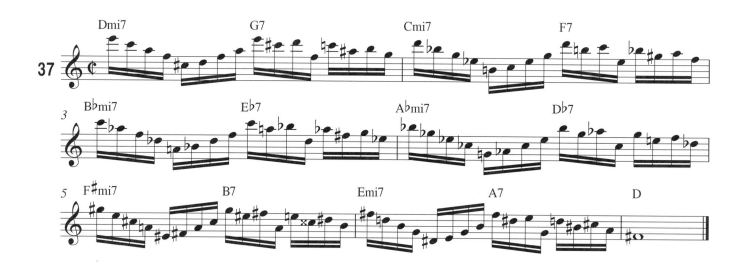

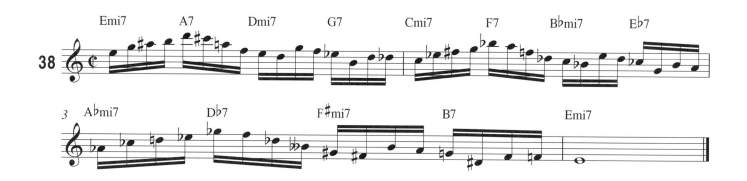

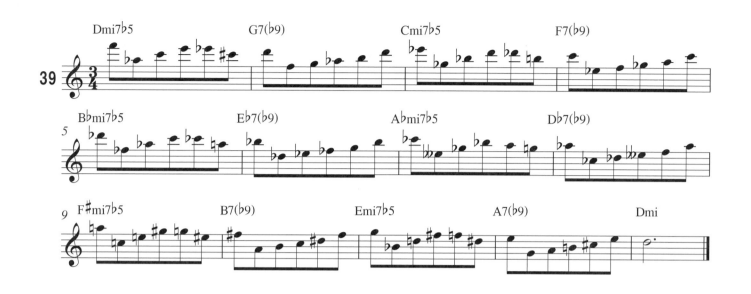

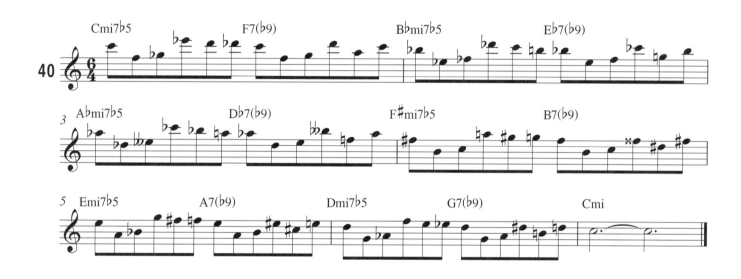

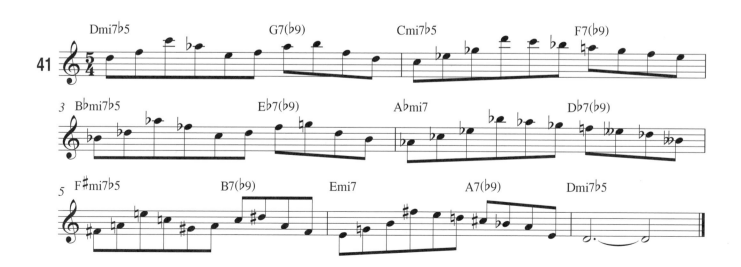

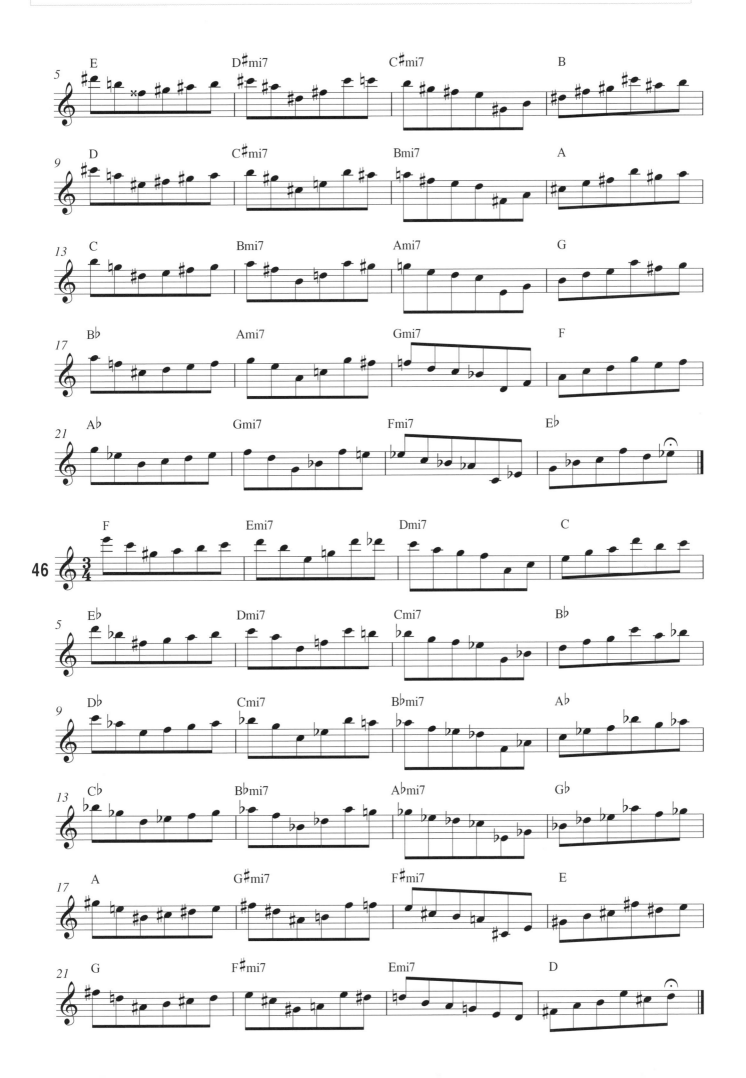

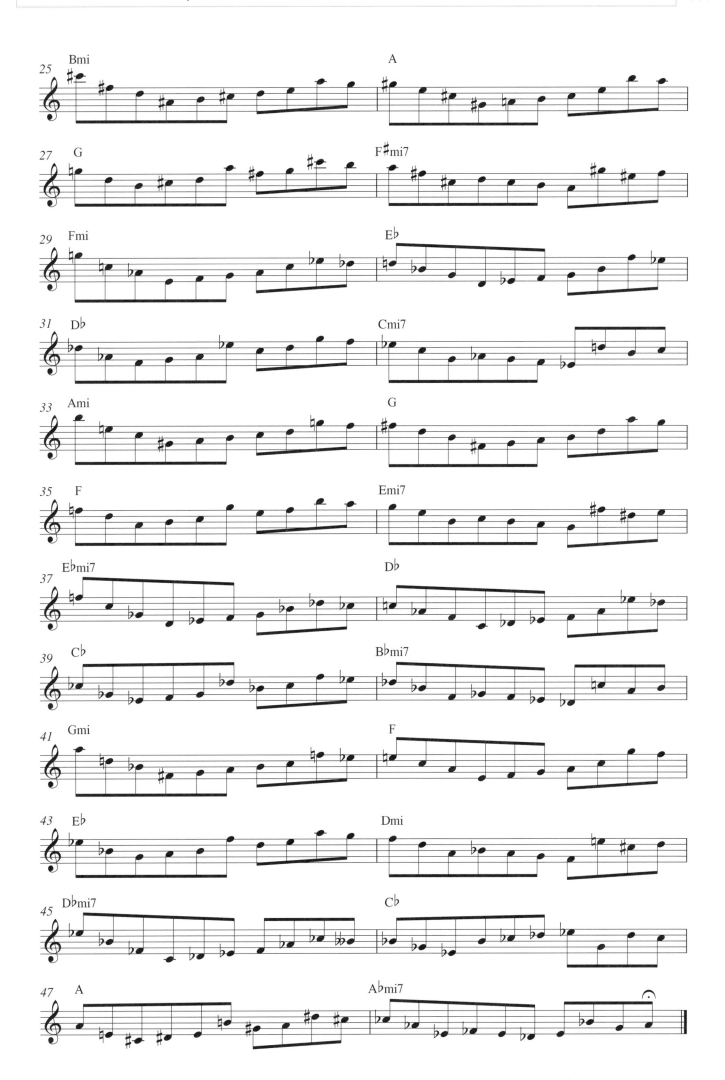

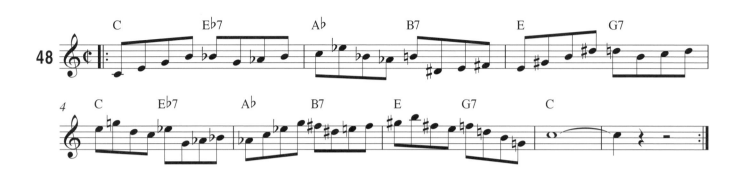

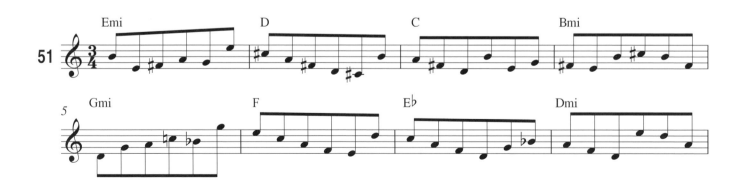

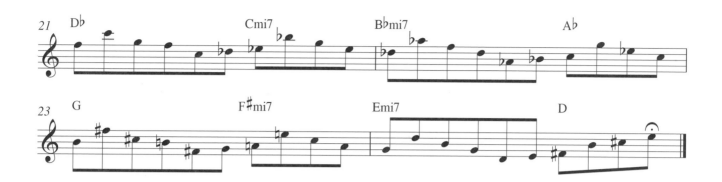

Rhythm Studies

"Rhythm Studies" provides the intermediate or advanced flutist with comprehensive reading experience in a variety of rhythmic styles and notational systems. The method is divided into four sections, and the following outline should assist the student in establishing an effective practice routine for each section.

SECTION I. SIMPLE METERS

The main purpose of the material is to provide rhythmic reading experience in simple time signatures. The notation is often deliberately complex and will familiarize the player with unconventional but often used forms of rhythmic notation as he acquires skill in reading syncopated rhythmic passages. The short duets illustrating the comparative notations used in 4/4 and 2/2 are important. The "A" and "B" portions of each example are the same. Only the notational system is different. Any comfortable tempo is acceptable and continued repetition of both parts of the duet is essential. Examples in 12/8 are to be played with the same interpretation as the related 4/4 examples.

NOTE: Only three types of articulation are used throughout the book:

$$= \text{long}$$
$$\wedge \quad = \text{short}$$
$$> \quad = \text{normal accent}$$

All other decisions regarding articulation and expression are at the discretion of the player.

SECTION II. COMPOUND METERS

This section begins with a series of short examples in a variety of simple and compound time signatures. Repeat each example until you are able to play it comfortably and gradually increase speed until you are able to read and interpret each example at any reasonable tempo. The extended etudes following these introductory exercises provide reading the experience in varying time signatures. Do not be intimidated by the frequent time signature changes. Count each bar but work toward feeling the "flow" of the music.

SECTION III. DOUBLE-TIME EXERCISES

These are "double-time" exercises in a variety of time signatures and you may initially find it necessary to work on isolated bars or phrases at very slow tempos. In Examples 1 through 6, note that the last two bars of each example are identical to the first four bars; only the pulse changes. In bars 1 through 4, count 4 to the bar; in bars 5 and 6, count 2 to the bar.

The concluding extended exercises and etudes incorporate characteristic double-time patterns. Again, each should be approached in a musical fashion and the double-time sections should be felt as an integral part of the compositional form.

SECTION IV. ETUDES

These concluding advanced etudes incorporate application of all of the rhythmic concepts developed in previous sections. In Etudes 12 through 15, a new concept is introduced and the following clarification may be helpful. After establishing the indicated metronome setting, simply remember that each bar occupies one metronome division, i.e. a bar of 5/4 occupies the same clock time duration as a bar of 3/4 (or 4/4 or 7/4 etc.).

Remember throughout the book that an awareness of both rhythmic notation and rhythmic interpretation are essential in developing reading skills. Interpretation is always at the discretion of the player and/or instructor and all exercises and etudes may (and should) be played in a variety of styles.

—Joseph Viola, 1974

Simple Meters

3A
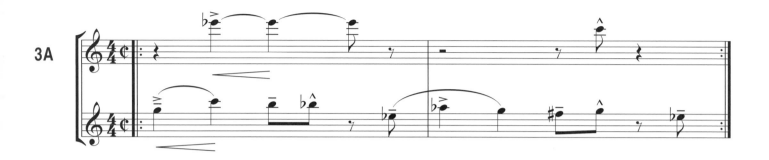

3B
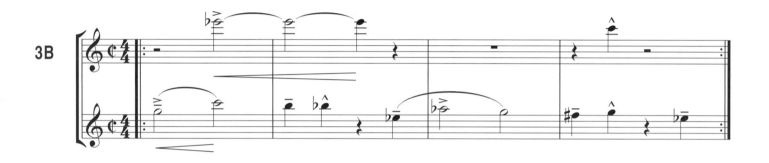

4A

4B

5A

5B

6A

6B

7A

7B

8A

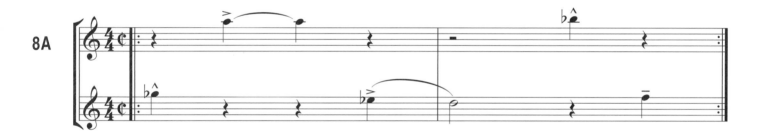

8B

9A

9B

10A

10B

11A

11B

12A

12B

13A

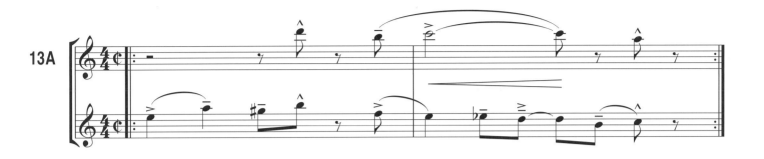

13B

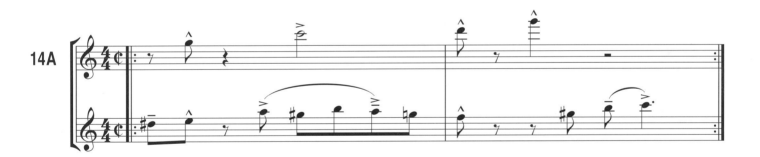

14A

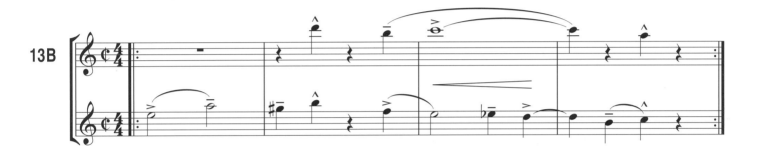

14B

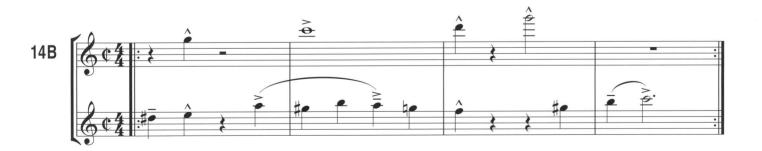

15A

15B

16A

16B

17A

17B
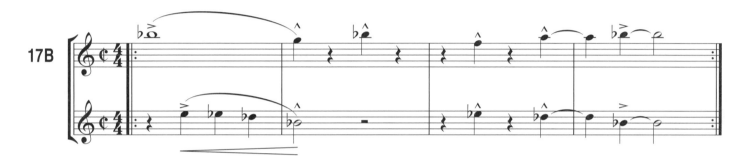

18A

18B

19A

19B

20A

20B

21A

21B

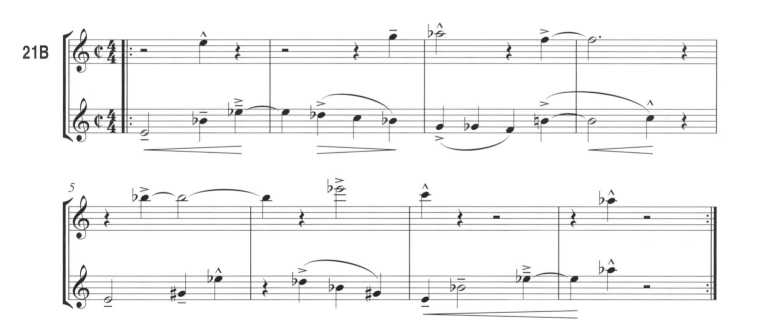

22A

22B

23A

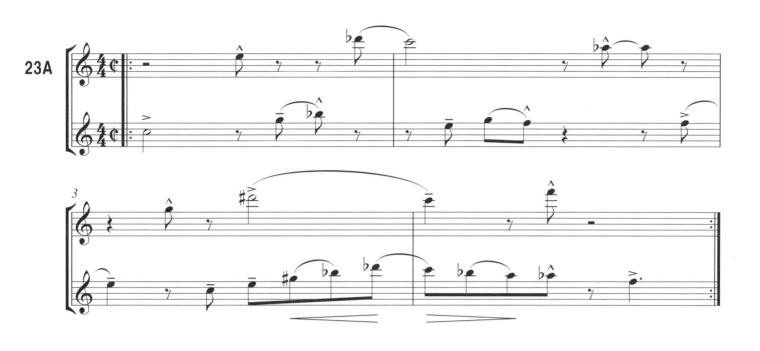

23B

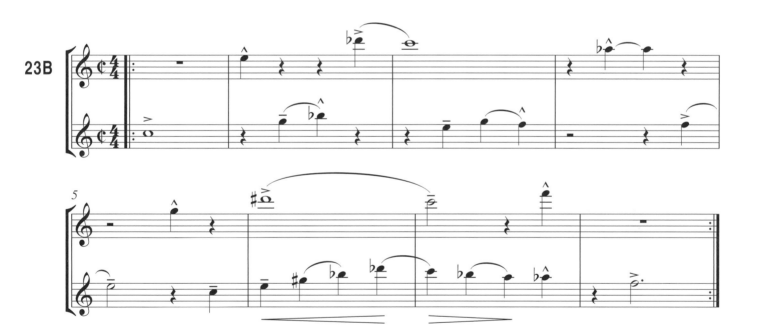

25A

25B

26A

26B

27A

27B

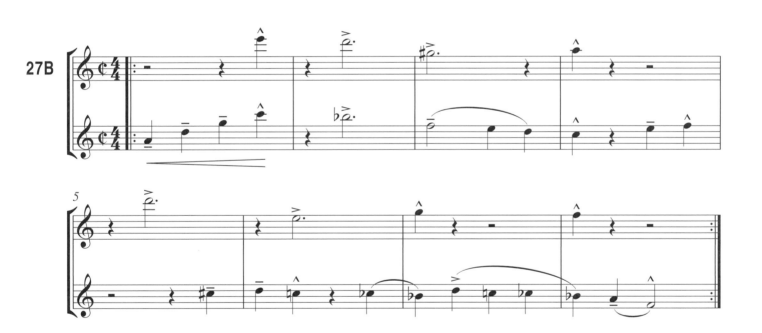

29A

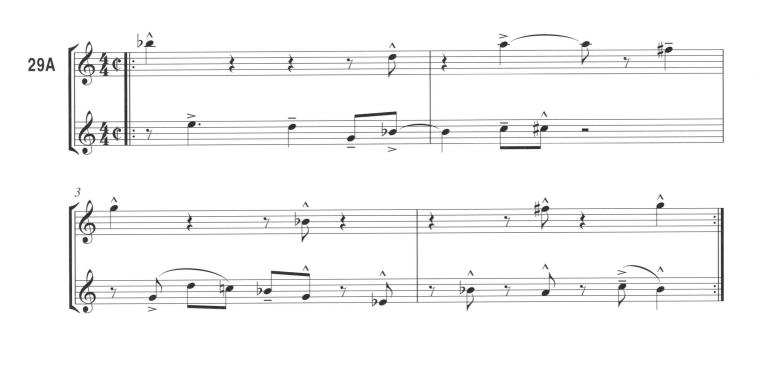

29B

30A

30B

32A

32B

34A

34B

36A

36B

37A

37B

38A

38B

39A

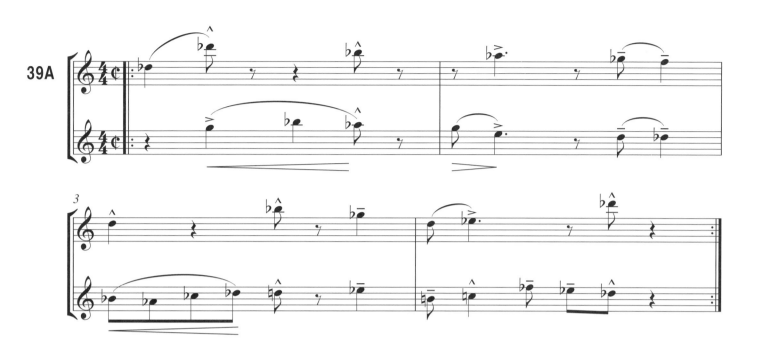

39B

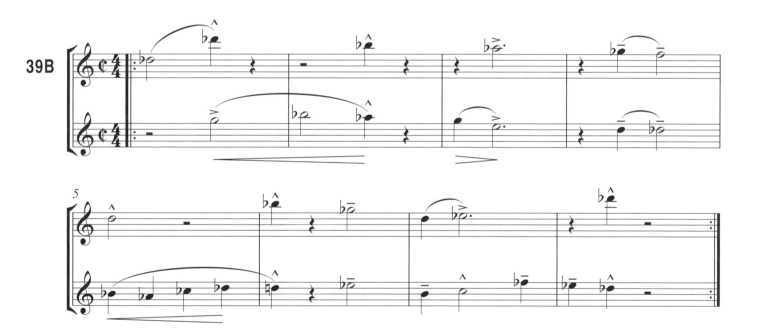

40A

40B

41A

41B

42A

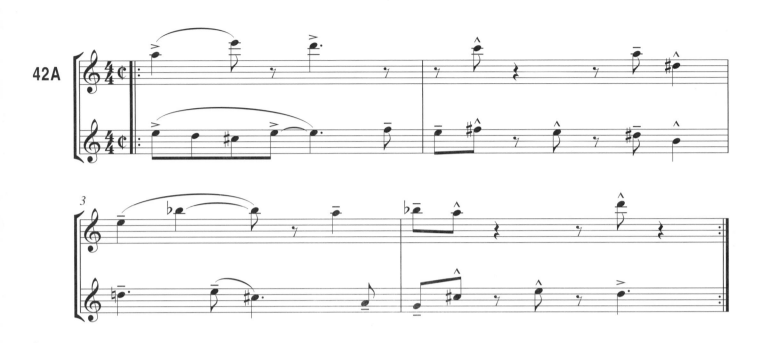

42B

43A

43B

44A

44B

45A

45B

46A

46B

49A

49B

50

51

53

68

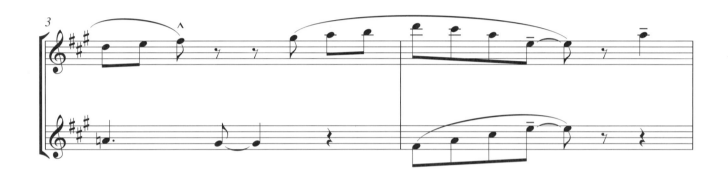

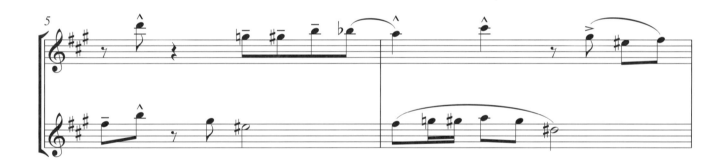

71

SECTION II

Simple and Compound Meters

Also practice these exercises an octave higher, where practical.

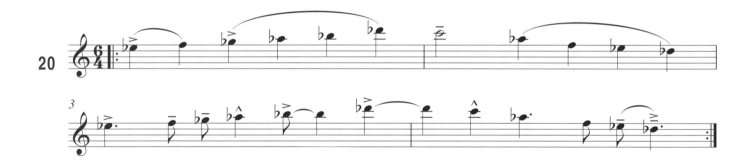

31

32

33

34

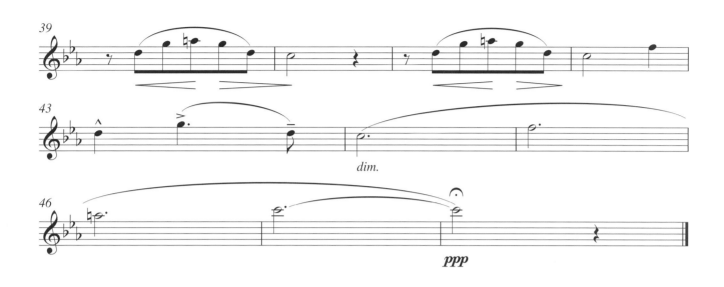

SECTION III

Double-Time Exercises

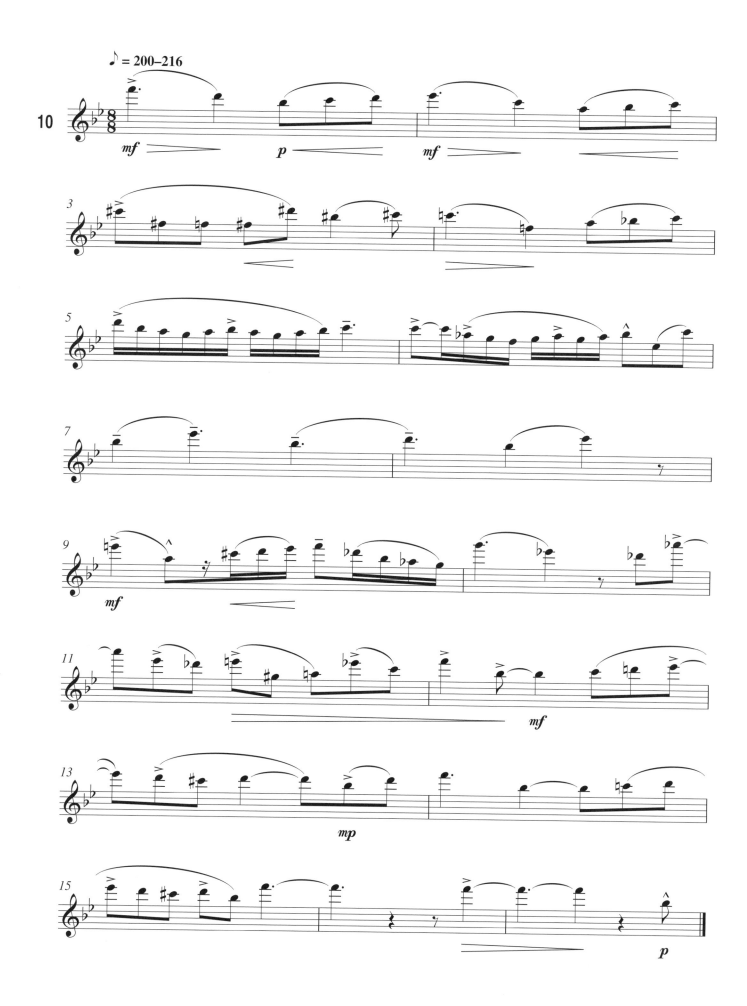

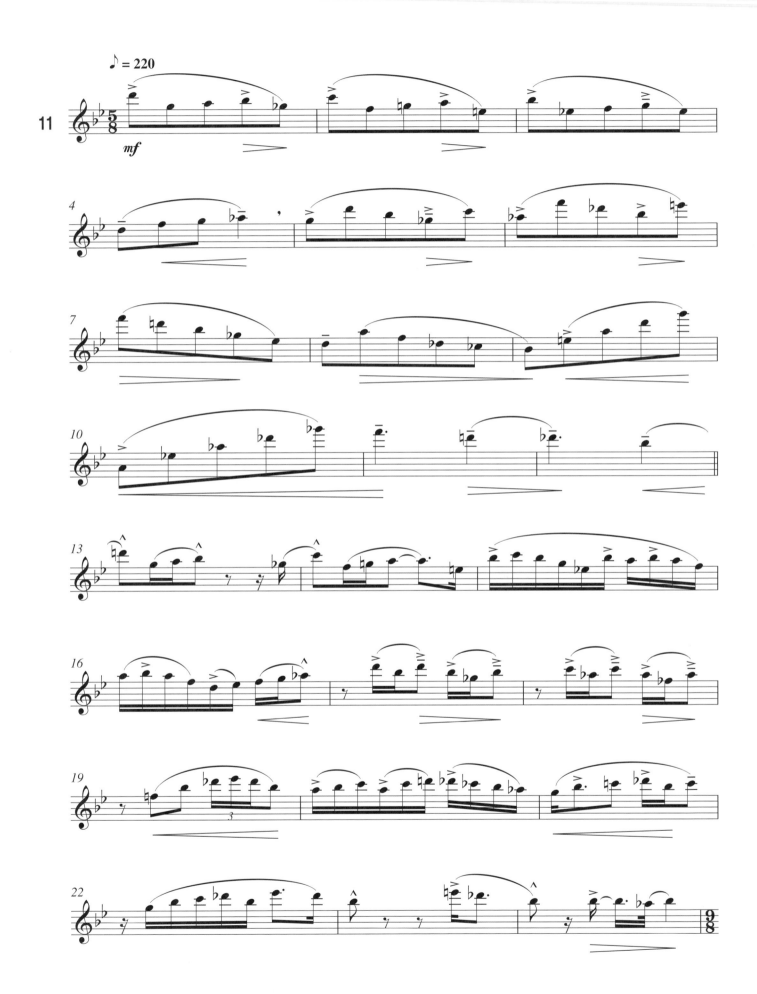

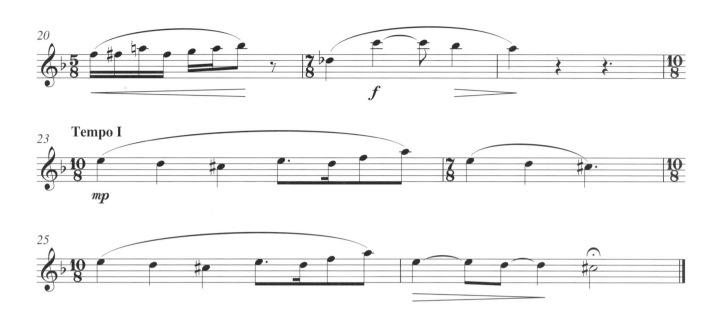

SECTION IV

Etudes

ETUDE NO. 1

ETUDE NO. 2

V.S.

ETUDE NO. 3

ETUDE NO. 4

ETUDE NO. 5

ETUDE NO. 6

V.S.

This page has been left blank intentionally.

ETUDE NO. 7

ETUDE NO. 8

ETUDE NO. 9

ETUDE NO. 10

ETUDE NO. 11

ETUDE NO. 12

ETUDE NO. 13

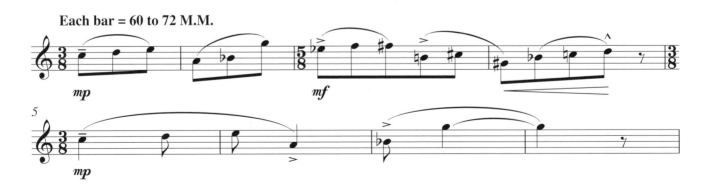

ETUDE NO. 14

ABOUT THE AUTHOR

Joseph E. Viola (1920 to 2001) was the founding chair of the Berklee College of Music Woodwind Department, and he taught at Berklee from shortly after its founding in 1947 until he retired in 1996. For most of the institution's first decade (and beyond), he taught theory, composition, saxophone, clarinet, flute, and the bulk of the ensembles.

Joe was a master woodwind player, and a mentor to thousands of musicians, including many of the most significant jazz artists and educators, such as Herb Pomeroy, Ray Santisi, Toshiko Akiyoshi, Charlie Mariano, Dick Nash, Sadao Watanabe, Quincy Jones, Joe Lovano, Walter Beasley, Jerry Bergonzi, Seamus Blake, Antonio Hart, Jane Ira Bloom, Richie Cole, Donald Harrison, Javon Jackson, Tommy Smith, George Garzone, Ernie Watts, Carol Chaikin, Jim Odgren, and Bill Pierce.

In World War II, he served as a sargeant, and performed in the Army Band. He went on to perform with Frank Sinatra, Lena Horne, the Shubert and Colonial Theater orchestras, the Boston Pops, and the BSO. Joe also founded the Berklee College Saxophone Quartet with John LaPorta, Harry Drabkin, and Gary Anderson, and he led that group to notable success.

He was a student of Benny Kanter (who played with Benny Goodman). Lawrence Berk (Berklee's founder and first president), Fernand Gillet (oboist of the Boston Symphony Orchestra), and saxophonist Marcel Mule.

Joe was the author of several seminal music method books, including the series *The Technique of the Saxophone, The Technique of the Flute*, and *Creative Studies.*

When he retired as chair of the Woodwind Department in 1985, the trustees of the college created a named scholarship endowment fund in his honor, and he was named Chair Emeritus of the Woodwind Department. He also received the Lifetime Achievement Award from the Massachusetts Music Educators Association, in recognition of his unique and enduring contributions to music education.